T[illegible] [illegible]ON

([illegible] E

London: HMSO

First published 1993

ISBN 0 11 341085 9

Acknowledgments

The authors would like to thank Terry Engelberg, John Miles, Gary Samson and Jan Lloyd, the research assistants on this project.

We would also like to thank Chief Superintendent Tom Williamson for his advice and assistance during this study.

This study would not have been possible without the cooperation of the officers at the eight stations featured in this report. We would especially like to thank the following people for their invaluable assistance and enthusiasm in helping with this study:

Chief Superintendent Syd Monk (Cumbria Constabulary)
Inspector Brian Minihane (Bedfordshire Constabulary)
Inspector Aidan MacAffee (Metropolitan Police)

Finally, we would like to thank Julie Vennard and Carol Hedderman from the Royal Commission.

The Authors

During the period of this research both authors were at the Institute of Social and Applied Psychology, University of Kent, Canterbury, CT2 7LZ. Stephen Moston is currently at the Department of Psychology, Deakin University, Geelong, Victoria, Australia 3217.

CONTENTS

		Page
Chapter 1:	**Introduction: Existing constraints and practice**	1
Chapter 2:	**Research Methodology and Sample of Cases**	11
Chapter 3:	**Survey Results**	19
Chapter 4:	**The Character of Interviews Outside the Police Station**	27
Chapter 5:	**Interviews Inside the Police Station**	33
Chapter 6:	**Discussion**	41
References		49
Appendix I:	Background to the Research Questionnaire	51
Appendix II:	The Research Questionnaire	53
Appendix III:	Statistical Analyses in Chapter 3	67
Appendix IV:	Statistical Analyses in Chapter 5	69

1
Introduction: Existing Constraints and Practice

The Police and Criminal Evidence Act 1984

The Police and Criminal Evidence Act 1984 (PACE) introduced new legislation governing the way in which suspects were arrested, detained and interviewed by police officers. The Act was intended to provide safeguards for both suspects and police officers. For example, Code C ensured that suspects were not subjected to undue pressure or oppression and made it difficult for the police to record inaccurately or invent the words used by the suspect in response to questioning (Heaton-Armstrong, 1989). For the benefit of police officers, the legislation was intended to make it difficult for a detained person to make unfounded allegations against the police, such as "verballing", which might otherwise have appeared credible.

One of the most important aspects of the new legislation governing the interviewing of suspects was the introduction of the tape recording of interviews inside the police station. Although many police officers were initially sceptical about the use of tape recording, it soon became readily accepted. This may have been due largely to the fact that tapes replaced the need for officers to record interviews contemporaneously (Williamson, 1990).

In their original form the Codes of Practice placed a number of controls on interviews inside the station, but were surprisingly vague about interviews conducted outside the police station. Some police officers who preferred to stick to the letter of the law, rather than its intention, found a number of loopholes which could be exploited (e.g., R. v. Vivian Parchment, 1989; R. v. Brezeanau and Francis, 1989). The problems concerning police malpractice in interviews therefore shifted away from the interview room to other locations, such as the police car en route to the station, where only contemporaneous notes (at best) could be kept (e.g., the case of *Hassan Khan*, cited in *The Independent*, February 24 1990).

Concerns about interviews outside the police station were voiced in a number of reports. For example, McConville and Morrell (1983) found that in Scotland many officers were routinely conducting interviews outside the police station. This was echoed by the Social Research Branch of the Scottish Home and Health Department report in 1985 (cited by Baldwin, 1985) which stated:

> We must be aware of the fact that if police officers are dramatically altering their practices when questioning suspects because of the introduction of tape recording by interviewing suspects either at the locus or in the police car on the way to the police station, but not on tape, they may give a veneer of success to the experiment whereas in reality the reverse may be the case (p.14).

More recently Dixon, Bottomley, Coleman, Gill and Wall (1990) also found evidence that undermined the apparent success of audio taping. Dixon et al. (p. 133) argued that "... there is the possibility that officers will try to evade recording and other controls by questioning suspects away from the interview room (at home during a post-arrest search, in the car on the way to the station, in the cells) or in the interview room before tape recording starts". The officer's task might then be to get the suspect to repeat relevant statements later in the formal taped interview.

Dixon et al. (1990) give one interesting example of such practices occurring entirely within the police station. In this case a suspect was taken to an interview room and asked a series of questions. He was then cautioned, and the recorded interview began, with the officer going over some of the matters previously discussed. The suspect protested: "I've told you about that already", to which the officer replied "Yes, but we have to get it formally now". When asked how often they clarified a suspect's account before starting an interview, 53 per cent of interviewed officers said always or often, while 28 per cent said rarely or never. The reason that statements are "clarified" prior to a recorded interview cannot always be attributed to the actions of police officers. Dixon et al. observed that some suspects would insist on "off the record" exchanges. In such exchanges the suspect might answer questions that later would only produce a reply of "No comment".

Wolchover and Heaton-Armstrong (1991a) argued that since PACE came into effect, police officers "have noticeably resorted to substantial questioning before arrival at the police station to an extent which used to be comparatively rare" (p.242). Qualifying this statement, they suggest that such questioning is most likely to be reported when, perhaps following legal advice, suspects decline to make any comment inside the police station. Baldwin (1990) suggested that if informal deals or agreements are worked out with suspects prior to the audio or video recording of the statement, then the benefits of such taping are lost.

Research suggesting that officers were evading the requirements of PACE and the Codes of Practice by "rule bending" have not been confined to interviews with suspects. According to Baldwin (1990) there is a considerable body of evidence to suggest that the provisions in the Act were "often only being followed in a cynical or half-hearted way" (p. 662). For example, suspects were being denied access to their solicitors and also being inadequately advised of their rights.

One notable example of rule bending was given by Sanders and Bridges (1990) who showed how officers, through a series of ploys (e.g., reading a person their rights at such a speed that they were incomprehensible), attempted to dissuade suspects from asking for legal advice. Sanders and Bridges are among those who have argued that police officers will try to circumvent PACE by holding interviews away from the interview room. In their research, officers spoke of "informal" visits to the cells to speak with suspects. This visit would not feature on the custody record, with custody officers seen as joining in the 'cover-up'. One of the officers questioned by Sanders and Bridges said that some other interviewing officers,

> ...feel guilty about going down there (to the cell). They're not so sure about whether it's right or wrong. You put it down on the custody record that you're explaining the man's position and then you go down there and treat it as an informal chat.

The custody record might subsequently show that the suspect had asked to speak to a particular detective, or that the officer had made a "welfare visit". Sanders and Bridges also suggest that the intentions behind informal chats are not solely confined to influencing admissions. On occasions the officer might want to collect information prior to the subsequent arrival of a solicitor, or even possibly to suggest that the request for legal advice is withdrawn. Sanders and Bridges do not see unlawful interrogation practices as occurring in the majority of cases, but simply those in which the police wish to circumvent legal advisors and other controls. At a broader level, they are also sceptical about the effects of PACE on police behaviour, concluding that,

> Police behaviour has been altered by legal changes, but not in the way intended. Only the *manner* in which the police secure their goals – putting maximum pressure on the suspects who matter most to them – has changed. Police malpractice has probably not been reduced but it has been made less overt, and hence more difficult to detect and control. In giving the false impression of complete police compliance with the law, unduly great faith in the police will now be encouraged. Thus PACE may, inadvertently, have made matters worse rather than better. (Sanders and Bridges, 1990, p.507)

The Revised Codes of Practice

The shortcomings of the original Codes of Practice resulted in a series of three draft revisions, circulated between August 1989 and November 1990

(Wolchover and Heaton-Armstrong, 1991a). The third and final draft was eventually accepted by Parliament in December 1990, becoming effective on April 1 1991. The new Codes included several revisions to the regulations concerning interviews with suspects outside the police station. Code C: 11.1 (p. 58) set out the following rules:

> Following a decision to arrest a suspect he must not be interviewed about the relevant offence except at a police station (or other authorised place of detention) unless the consequent delay would be likely:
>
> (a) to lead to interference with or harm to evidence connected with an offence or interference with or physical harm to other persons; or
> (b) to lead to the alerting of other persons suspected of having committed an offence but not yet arrested for it; or
> (c) to hinder the recovery of property obtained in consequence of the commission of an offence.
>
> Interviewing in any of these circumstances should cease once the relevant risk has been averted or the necessary questions have been put in order to avert that risk.

The revised Codes also make it clear that every interview that takes place must be recorded, regardless of where the interview took place. Code C:11.5 (p. 59) states that,

> (b) The record must state the place of the interview, the time it begins and ends, the time the record is made (if different), any breaks in the interview and the names of all those present; and must be made on the forms provided for this purpose or in the officer's pocket-book or in accordance with the code of practice for the tape-recording of police interviews with suspects.
>
> (c) The record must be made during the course of the interview, unless in the investigating officer's view this would not be practicable or would interfere with the conduct of the interview, and must constitute either a verbatim record of what has been said, or failing this, an account of the interview which adequately and accurately summarises it.

Under C:11.13 officers are now also obliged to record any comments made by the suspected person, including unsolicited remarks, which are outside the context of an interview but which might be relevant to the offence.

The Notes for Guidance in Code C (11A; p. 60) offer a further clarification of the law, making a clear distinction between the separate activities of *questioning* and *interviewing*.

> An interview is the questioning of a person regarding his involvement or suspected involvement in a criminal offence or offences. Questioning a person only to obtain information or his explanation of the facts or in the ordinary course of the officer's duties does not constitute an interview for the purpose of this code. Neither does questioning which is confined to the proper and effective conduct of a search.

In the Codes the procedure of *questioning* a potential suspect is quite distinct from *interviewing*. A key consequence of the difference between these two forms of encounter with suspects is that interviews must be recorded, whereas there are no such controls on questioning. However, if a suspect should make an admission or other form of damaging statement in response to *questioning*, then the officer concerned should make a record of that statement and caution the suspect. Although *interviewing* outside the station is effectively outlawed, there is a strong need for officers to conduct *questioning*. For example, if a person were found in possession of a knife in a public place, that person should be questioned in order to establish whether or not a crime had been committed. It is possible that the person might have a logical and honest explanation for the presence of the knife. The offence 'possession of an offensive weapon' can only be determined through *questioning*. Similarly, in a number of other offences (e.g., theft) it is often impossible to assert whether or not a crime has been committed without hearing the suspect's explanation. Consequently it is clearly intended that in certain circumstances officers should question suspects.

The revised Codes of Practice have not been an unqualified success in redefining interviews outside the police station. Several commentators have raised doubts as to how effective the codes would be in practice. Wolchover and Heaton-Armstrong (1991b) suggested that the ban on *interviews* between the decision to arrest and arrival at the police station sounded "the death knell" for most "car seat" interviews, although they anticipated that officers would try to stretch the definitions of exceptional circumstances, with "imaginative officers dreaming up all manner of ingenious pretexts" (p.243). Greaves and Pickover (1991) proposed that the notes of guidance would go some way towards resolving the question of what constitutes an "interview", although they felt that the term "explanation of the facts" was somewhat ambiguous and the position on listening to a suspect and passing an occasional observation remained uncertain.

Wolchover and Heaton-Armstrong (1991b) give an example of the potential problems that might arise from the new codes in the hypothetical case of an officer who comes across a man holding a bloody knife, standing over a lifeless body. In their interpretation of the revised Codes, Wolchover and Heaton-Armstrong (1991b) claim that the officer would be expected to arrest the man and it would not be until they had arrived at the station before the suspect could be asked "What happened?". In this and other examples, Wolchover and Heaton-Armstrong (1991a; 1991b) raise a number of questions concerning the arguments that will follow from the new legislation. They insist that in effectively outlawing interviews outside the police station, the Home Office has "thrown the baby out with the bath water" and abandoned a potentially important component of the investigative process. The suspect's first reaction to arrest, they argue, may be of crucial importance and they put forward a strong case for the use of portable tape recorders, a suggestion which will be considered below.

The formal distinction made by the Codes of Practice between *questioning* and *interviewing* will be recognised in this Report by italicising those terms where they are used in ways which seem to reflect the Codes' intention. Of course, *questioning* and *interviewing* themselves take place in the context of a developing encounter with the suspect. Other conversations with the suspect may flesh out the total interaction and may both affect and be affected by the overall character of the interactions. We, therefore, made some attempt in this study to assess the importance of the role played by non-offence related conversations outside the interviewing room in the police station.

It should perhaps be noted at this point that "interviews outside the police station" are strictly speaking those interviews which take place "outside the designated interview room". That is a tiresome phrase, and we shall stick to "outside the police station" while recognising that a small number of these interviews (6 in all) actually took place in the police station but not in the "designated interview room" (see Table 10).

The use of tape recorders outside the police station

The restrictions placed on interviews outside the police station have arisen largely because of the potential for disputes over the accuracy of what was said. One method for ensuring the accuracy of statements made outside the police station is to extend the use of tape recording equipment and to issue officers with portable tape recorders. The accuracy of any statements could then be verified. Wolchover and Heaton-Armstrong (1991a; 1991b) advocate the use of portable tape recorders and report that some officers are already carrying them, albeit covertly, to protect themselves against later complaint.

Heaton-Armstrong (1989) suggested that the importance of the evidence gathered at the time of an arrest is an argument in favour of the use of tape recording. For example, a guilty suspect may be more likely to "get it off his chest" on first contact with the police, but stay silent upon arrival at the police station. Wolchover and Heaton-Armstrong (1991a; 1991b) do not simply raise the future *possibility* of using portable tape recorders, they are clearly advocating that officers should start to use such equipment now. For example, they state:

> We can see no legal objection to the use of hand-held tape recorders and suggest that prudent officers might start using them now without waiting for approval from above. For those who, understandably, do not feel sufficiently courageous to follow this course, we advocate a much more cautious approach to the endorsement by suspects of written interview records compiled after the event. (1991b; p.753)

Apart from those officers who carry tape recorders covertly for self-protection, there are clearly occasions in which the use of portable tape recorders is officially sanctioned. One striking illustration of the potential of portable tape recorders came to light in the fraud trial of Ambrose Mendy (Independent, 19 April 1991; p.5), as is outlined below.

> Detectives who made a dawn raid on the home of a boxing promoter accused of a £650,000 fraud conspiracy used a concealed tape recorder to capture conversations....
> A transcript of a tape.... showed that in the chaos Mr Mendy had called his wife 'Jen' repeatedly as he tried to contact his lawyer and mind the children....
> Earlier in the trial Mr Mendy denied using that abbreviation of Jennifer to address his wife, though he occasionally called her Jenny. But yesterday under cross-examination.... he 'could not deny' the words when confronted with the transcript.
> The prosecution alleges that a letter and note addressed to 'Jen', found in the guest bedroom cabinet of his Wanstead home, and seized for handwriting comparisons were by him. He had denied writing them and the use of the name 'Jen'.
> The letter and note, along with other documents which the police say were written by him.... were a 'fraudsters' index' corresponding to companies targeted for the attempted fraud.

In the Mendy case there appears to have been no problem in court with the introduction of the tape recorded interview as evidence, thereby supporting the suggestions of Wolchover and Heaton-Armstrong.

It should also be noted that there is another side to this debate, namely the carrying of portable tape recorders by *suspects*. Just as officers may be carrying tape recorders as protection, so too might suspects. This clearly would not be expected to occur with any degree of frequency, but it is a possibility which should be kept in mind.

Predicting the outcome of interviews with suspects

In a recent paper, Moston, Stephenson and Williamson (1992a) outlined a model of how the characteristics of a suspect (e.g., age, criminal history) and case (e.g., offence type, strength of evidence), interacted with police interviewing styles to affect the outcome of interviews. The decision to admit an allegation during interviewing was found to be primarily associated with three factors: strength of evidence (number of admissions increases with greater strength of evidence), legal advice (fewer admissions following legal advice and a greater incidence of the right to silence) and the criminal history of the suspect (fewer admissions from those with prior criminal convictions). In that article it was argued that there were few links between case characteristics and police interviewing tactics, with officers displaying a restricted range of interviewing styles. It was suggested that in the vast majority of cases in which confessions were made, police interviewing techniques played virtually no part in influencing the decision making of the suspect. In most cases officers adopted bland non-confrontational interviewing techniques and rarely resorted to any overtly persuasive questioning. The suspect's decision to either admit or deny an allegation appeared to have been determined before the start of the tape recorded interview. A further observation in this study was that suspects rarely ever changed their statements (e.g., from denial to admission) during the course of interviewing.

The suggestion that suspects have already decided whether or not to make an admission at the outset of interviewing has important implications for the present study. It was assumed by Moston et al. (1992a) that police interviewing techniques were largely ineffective, but this conclusion may have been mistaken. As has already been discussed, there is a great deal of scope for officers to have 'discussions' with suspects prior to the start of a taped interview. Such discussions might occur at the crime scene, on the way to the station, in the custody suite, in the cells, in the corridors on the way to the interview room, or even in the interview room itself, just before the tape recorder is switched on. It is possible that in such discussions police officers might effectively manipulate the decision making of suspects in ways which are not readily detectable from the tape recorded interviews.

The current study will attempt to expand upon our earlier research by incorporating details of the arrests of suspects, as well as questioning, interviewing and other forms of conversation, into an analysis of why suspects make admissions.

The current study

The current study is an examination of the extent to which suspects are questioned and interviewed outside the police station and the effects of such encounters on any subsequent interviews inside the police station. The entire study had to be conducted between September 1991 and March 1992 to fit in with the Royal Commission's research timetable. The restricted amount of time available meant that it was impossible to follow a series of cases through the entire criminal justice system in order to determine the importance of any encounters outside the police station on the prosecution and conviction of suspects. Our restricted aims were as follows:

1. To determine the extent of *questioning* and *interviewing* and other forms of conversation outside the police station and the case factors associated with each form of police-suspect encounter.

2. To examine the purpose of interviews conducted outside the police station, the records kept and the information gathered.

3. To determine the association between encounters outside the station and the outcome of interviews inside the police station and the decision to charge or release.

2
Research Methodology and Sample of Cases

This Chapter describes the development of the research design employed in this study. The potential sensitivity of the subject matter meant that care had to be taken in order to ensure the cooperation of the police forces involved. A questionnaire based study was designed to record details of all cases occurring during specified time periods. The sample of cases featuring in this report is described in the final part of the Chapter.

The development of the research methodology

The topic of this research project is undoubtedly a contentious aspect of current policing. Even though there has been an upsurge in research on police interviewing, this has been confined to interviews within the police station. Similarly, the provision of police interview techniques training courses and materials has, until only recently, almost exclusively focused on interviews inside the station.

In attempting to carry out research on interviewing practices outside the police station it was necessary to conduct extensive negotiations with police officers (of all ranks). These preliminary discussions helped to determine the aims, methodology and scope of the present report. It is important to note that the current authors have previously conducted several studies on police interviewing procedures,and the police service has already incorporated ideas from this research (e.g., procedures for questioning suspects who use the right of silence) into training. This background meant that obtaining access to various police forces was relatively straightforward. Senior officers were approached directly and permission to carry out studies was readily given. Having easily cleared the first hurdle of gaining access, the next stage of the research was to speak with the officers who would actually be participating in this research.

Upon our announcing the idea of the study at one station (in the Metropolitan area) where pilot work was undertaken, one officer immediately stated "We don't do interviews outside the station". This attitude was subsequently encountered in discussions with officers at other stations. The most plausible explanation for statements of this kind is that some officers are very anxious to defend themselves against possible criticism. Officers of different type and rank are aware that interviews outside the police station are not generally supposed to occur, and are not entirely clear about the circumstances in which interviews are permitted. The current research topic bears upon legislation that is clearly not fully understood or consistently interpreted.

A key concern during the negotiations was that some officers might be reluctant to participate if there was any likelihood of their responses in the questionnaire being used against them, either by defence lawyers or by their own senior officers. To solve this problem it was made clear throughout the study that the survey results would be kept confidential. The issue of confidentiality was particularly pertinent to some of the questions asked of officers, for example, those concerned with the use of personal tape recorders. As was suggested in Chapter 1, it does appear that a number of officers are carrying concealed tape recorders. In contrast to the practice of covert taping in planned operations, the resulting tapes are almost certainly only used to prevent future disciplinary action following accusations of misconduct. The tapes are not forming part of the official record of interviews/arrests.

Although some concerns were voiced, overall there were remarkably few problems in implementing the study. The most prevalent attitude towards the research was one of curiosity about current practices. In each of the three forces officers were appointed to act as liaisons for the research project: the assistance of these officers was crucial to the running of the study.

The research questionnaire

Data were collected using a three-part questionnaire attached to custody records at participating stations. Each time a suspect was brought into custody and a custody record was issued, a corresponding questionnaire was administered. Each part of the questionnaire was designed to be completed at a set point in the investigation. The first part of the questionnaire (Form A) asked about the circumstances of arrest, the characteristics of the suspect and details of any questioning or interviewing outside the police station. Form B focused on interviews inside the police station. The third part of the questionnaire (Form C) considered the action to be taken against the suspect (e.g., charge or release) and the importance of interviews and other forms of evidence in influencing this decision. The questionnaire was designed to be as straightforward to complete as possible. A large number of the questions simply required officers to tick appropriate responses. A full copy of the research questionnaire is included in Appendix I, preceded by a description of the questionnaire structure and procedure to be followed at each participating police station.

The research sample

Periods of data collection at each station

The research questionnaires were completed in eight police stations (listed below in Table 1). Three of the stations were from the Cumbria Constabulary, three from Bedfordshire Constabulary and two from the Metropolitan Police.

Form A was completed by the arresting officer in each case. The form was completed either immediately upon arrival at the station, or as soon as possible afterwards. Form B was concerned with the interviewing of suspects inside the police station and was completed by interviewing officers following completion of an interview. Details of each interview with the suspect were recorded separately. Space was provided for details of up to three interviews. If more than three interviews took place then officers were requested to continue on a specifically designed continuation sheet (Supplementary Form B) which was available from the custody officer. Form C of the questionnaire was completed either by the interviewing officer, or more commonly by the custody officer, after a decision had been reached on whether or not to charge the suspect.

The dates at which data collection at each station started and finished are listed below in Table 1. The total numbers of custody records issued during these periods and the number of criminal offences for which research questionnaires were completed, are also shown. Questionnaires were not completed for public order offences (e.g., drunk and disorderly).

Table 1
Periods of data collection and number of questionnaires completed

Force Station	Date Started	Date Finished	Total No. Custody Records Issued	Total No. and Percentage of Criminal Offences
Cumbria				
Barrow	27.10.91	10.11.91	155	81 (52%)
Workington	27.10.91	10.11.91	88	63 (72%)
Carlisle	27.10.91	10.11.91	235	127 (54%)
Bedfordshire				
Dunstable	11.11.91	25.11.91	85	62 (73%)
Bedford	11.11.91	25.11.91	114	77 (68%)
Luton	11.11.91	25.11.91	100	79 (79%)
*Metropolitan**				
Edmonton	27.11.91	12.12.91	57	43 (75%)
Tottenham	27.12.91	11.12.91	–	109 –
Total				641

(* Note: (i) At Edmonton the study ran for only eight hours a day over seven days. (ii) At Tottenham the number of custody records issued is not known exactly, but we believe that the percentage of offences covered was higher than average).

The suspects

The characteristics of the suspects featured in this study were as follows. There were 548 males (85.5%) and 93 females (14.5%). 499 suspects were Caucasian (77.8%), whilst the others were from minority ethnic groups, as follows: Afro-Caribbean (85 cases), Indian (25 cases), or of other ethnic groups (29 cases). In three cases information on ethnic group was missing.

Other characteristics of the suspects include the following: 455 suspects (71%) were unemployed. 373 of the 641 suspects (61.1%) had previous criminal convictions, whereas 237 (38.9%) did not (data being missing in 31 cases). In 8 cases (1.2%) the suspect was known to have some form of "mental handicap" and in a further 7 cases (1.1%) the arresting officer had reason to suspect that the suspect *might* be mentally handicapped. The suspects were aged between 11 and 81 years of age. 104 suspects were aged 16 or under.

The offences

Table 2 shows the types of offences about which the suspects were questioned. The list is only concerned with a single main offence for each suspect, even though some suspects were questioned about multiple offences. The Table divides offences into the two categories of property and person offences.

Table 2
Numbers of offence types

Offence	No. of Cases
Abduction	1
Actual Bodily Harm	36
Arson	7
Assault	34
Burglary	93
Criminal Damage	61
Deception/Fraud	33
Drugs (Possession/supply)	33
Going Equipped	12
Grievous Bodily Harm	10
Handling Stolen Goods	24
Incest	1
Indecent Assault	5
Murder/Attempted Murder	2
Rape	5
Robbery	17
TDA/TWOC (Car Theft)	55
Threats to Kill	3
Theft	179
Theft from Automobile	18
Possession of offensive weapons	12
Total	641

The vast majority of offences were against property (about 85%), with theft and burglary the two largest single types of offence. There were relatively few person offences, which included 11 sexual offences. The arresting officers were asked to rate the severity of the offences. 122 cases (19.2%) were classed as trivial, 387 (61.0%) as moderately serious, and 126 (19.8%) as very serious. Ratings of severity were missing in six cases.

The arrests

The arresting officers were predominantly police constables (505 cases: 78.8%). Police Sergeants made arrests on 13 occasions (2.0%); Detective Constables made arrests in 105 cases (16.4%) and Detective Sergeants in 12 cases (1.9%). In five cases (0.9%) arrests were made by Special Constables. Table 3 shows the locations at which suspects were arrested.

Table 3
Numbers and percentages of locations where suspects were arrested

Arrest Location	Number of Arrests	Percentage of Arrests
At Police Station	89	13.9
At Crime Scene	297	46.5
At Home/Residence of Suspect	167	26.1
In Street (Not Crime Scene)	74	11.6
At Home of Friend	6	0.9
At Work	6	0.9
Missing	2	–
Total	641	

Not surprisingly, the largest number of arrests were made at the scene where the crime had been committed. A large number of arrests (about a quarter) were made at the home or place of residence of suspects.

Table 4 shows the types of people who were present at the time that the suspect was arrested. In some cases more than one person was present.

Table 4
Numbers and percentages of other persons present at the time of arrest

Others Present At Arrest	Number of Arrests[1]	Percentage of Arrests
Legal Representative	59	9.2
Appropriate Adult	80	12.5
Independent Witness	15	2.3
Victim	16	2.5
Store Detective	29	4.5
Social Services/Care Staff	10	1.6
Family of Suspect	39	6.1
Other Suspects	65	10.1
Friend of Suspect	33	5.1
General Public	5	0.8

[1] Data refer to 311 cases. More than one category of person was present in a number of instances.

It was interesting to note that some suspects were arrested in the presence of either a solicitor (about 9%) or an appropriate adult (12.5%). In these cases the arrest location was typically at the police station or at the home/place of residence of the suspect. Very few arrests were made in the presence of either an independent eyewitness or the victim of the offence. Obviously, in some cases, there was more than one other person present, whilst in some cases there was no other person present. In fact, a total of 330 suspects (51.5%) was arrested at a time and location when there was no other person present.

3
Survey Results

Chapter 3 examines the incidence and circumstances of *questioning* prior to arrest, *interviews* outside the police station and non-offence related conversations prior to arrival at the station. Details of the statistical analysis carried out on these data are reported in Appendix III. All associations between variables discussed in this report reach conventional levels of statistical significance.

The *questioning* of suspects prior to arrest

Of the 641 suspects in the survey, 201 (31 per cent) were reportedly questioned prior to their arrest. In 154 (77%) cases in which suspects were questioned the purpose was to establish whether or not a crime had been committed. The other main reason was to eliminate the suspect from enquiries (42 cases, 21%). In five cases (2%) the suspect was initially seen as a potential eyewitness.

The data from the present study were analyzed using log linear analysis. The rationale for this technique and the full statistical results for this chapter are included in Appendix III. Table A in Appendix III lists the results of the analysis of variables linked to the *questioning* of suspects outside the police station. In the analysis it was necessary to collapse some data categories in order to make the results more meaningful. The need for this procedure is discussed in Appendix III.

The analysis showed that four variables were independently linked to *questioning* and there was a single interaction effect between two variables. Police force, ethnic group of suspect, location of arrest and the existence of other suspects were each linked to the occurrence of *questioning*. Each of these four variables will be discussed in turn.

The incidence of questioning and the locations where questioning took place

Table 5 shows the locations at which *questioning* took place. The vast majority of *questioning* prior to arrest took place at crime scenes (61% of the 201 cases) or at the home of the suspect (about 19% of the 201 cases). About 12% of suspects were questioned inside the police station. *Questioning* inside police cars was very rare (only 2 cases). This is hardly surprising as the presence of the suspect inside a police car would suggest that a decision to arrest has been made. The effect of location of arrest was significantly associated with *questioning* (x^2 = 10.415; d.f. = 3; p<.05)

Table 5
The locations at which *questioning* prior to arrest took place

Location of *Questioning*	Number and Percentage of Cases in Which *Questioning* Took Place	
Police Station	25	12.4%
Crime Scene	123	61.2%
Home/Residence/work	38	18.9%
In Street (Not Crime Scene)	11	5.5%
By telephone	1	0.5%
In prison	1	0.5%

The Incidence of Questioning in Each Police Force

There was a considerable degree of variation in the amount of questioning carried out in each of the three forces. Table 6 shows (in bold type) how the incidence of *questioning* varied between the three forces featured in this study. The levels of *questioning* range from a low of 21% in Bedfordshire to a high of 52% in the Metropolitan stations (x^2 = 37.243; d.f. = 2; p<.0001). Questioning in the Metropolitan Police occurs significantly more frequently than it does in Cumbria or Bedfordshire. The figures for the two county forces are not significantly different. Included within Table 6 are the corresponding figures for each of the eight stations featured in the study.

Table 6
The incidence of *questioning* prior to arrest in each police force

Force / Station	Number of Cases	Number and Percentage of Cases in Which *Questioning* Took Place	
Cumbria	**271**	**76**	**28.0%**
Barrow	81	24	29.6%
Workington	63	7	11.1%
Carlisle	127	45	35.4%
Bedfordshire	**218**	**46**	**21.1%**
Dunstable	62	11	17.7%
Bedford	77	15	19.5%
Luton	79	20	25.3%
Metropolitan	**152**	**79**	**52.0%**
Edmonton	43	21	48.8%
Tottenham	109	58	53.2%

The incidence of questioning and the ethnic group of suspects

In the survey suspects were classified according to their ethnic group. The majority of suspects were Caucasian, whilst others were Afro-Caribbean, Asian, or of other groups. The analysis showed an effect of race of suspect on questioning (x^2 = 17.421; d.f.= 3; p<.001).

Table 7 below shows that Caucasian and Asian suspects were less likely to be questioned prior to arrest than Afro-Caribbean suspects. The difference held in all 3 police forces and in all of the offences where the numbers were sufficient for comparison.

Table 7
Ethnic group of suspect and *questioning* prior to arrest

Ethnic Group of Suspect	No. of Cases	Number and Percentage of Cases in Which *Questioning* Took Place	
Caucasian	499	140	28.1%
Afro-Caribbean	85	43	50.6%
Asian	25	07	28.0%
Other Minority Ethnic group	29	11	37.9%
Missing	03	–	–

The incidence of questioning and the existence of other suspects

Table 8 shows the incidence of questioning in cases in which there were suspects other than the person arrested. This shows that *questioning* was slightly more common when only one person was suspected of having committed an offence (x^2 = 5.844; d.f. = 1; p<.05). This may simply reflect a practical constraint on *questioning* in that if there are multiple suspects who have been identified at the same time it is unlikely that an officer will want to initiate any form of discussion, preferring instead to isolate the suspects in order to question them separately.

Table 8
Other suspects and questioning prior to arrest

Existence of Other Suspects	Number of Cases	Number and Percentage of Cases in Which *Questioning* Took Place	
No Others Suspected	304	107	35.2%
Others Suspected	337	94	27.9%

There was a statically significant interaction between the ethnic group of the suspect, the existence of other suspects and the incidence of questioning (x^2 = 4.696; d.f. = 1; p<.05). Table 7 had shown that non-

Caucasian suspects – and most particularly Afro-Caribbean suspects – were more likely to be questioned that Caucasians, whilst Table 8 had shown that when there are other suspects, questioning is generally less likely to occur. When there were no other suspects, Caucasians are somewhat more likely to be questioned (34% of cases) than when there are other suspects (24%). However, for non-Caucasians questioning is more likely when there are other suspects (47% of cases) as compared to when there are no other suspects (41% of cases).

The interviewing of suspects outside the police station

A total of 52 of the 641 suspects (8.1%) was *interviewed* prior to arrival at the police station. 30 of these suspects (57.7%) were *questioned* prior to the interview. In 20 of the 52 cases (38.5%) the interview was initiated by a police officer, in 29 cases (55.8%) the suspect initiated the interview and in 3 cases (5.8%) the interview was seen as being initiated by another person. That is, the statement of a third party, such as a store detective prompted the police officer or suspect to say something that then initiated an interview.

Table 9 below shows the locations in which the *interviewing* took place. Interviews took place primarily at the crime scene or in a police car on the way to the station. as noted earlier, 6 of the interviews conducted 'outside the police station' were in fact, conducted inside the station but outside the interview room. In one case the interview took place in the private car of an off-duty officer who had witnessed an accident involving a stolen car.

Table 9
The locations where *interviewing* occurred

Location of *Interview*	Number of Cases	Percentage of Cases
Crime Scene	23	44.2%
In Police Car	13	25.0%
In Police Station	6	11.5%
Home of Suspect	7	13.5%
Private Car of Police Officer	1	1.9%
In Street (Not Crime Scene)	1	1.9%
Car of Suspect	1	1.9%

Table 10 below shows the reasons officers gave for the 52 interviews. In 23% of cases officers gave as the reason 'to establish the person's involvement in an offence. This is in accordance with the Notes of Guidance to Code C (see page 6 of the current report). In one case an interview was conducted to identify other suspects.

One of the reasons cited (to identify whether or not a crime had occurred), are properly covered under the definition of *questioning* rather than *interviewing*. The reason "to gather evidence" is very imprecise. In a number of cases it was allegedly the suspect who initiated the interview, either by asking what would happen to them, or by making some other statement. The one case in which an interview developed out of a non-offence related conversation occurred when a suspect arrested in another force was being driven to one of the forces in the study. The contents of the 52 interviews will be returned to in greater detail in Chapter 4.

Table 10
The reasons for *interviews* (outside the police station)

Reason For *Interview*	Number of Cases	Percentage of Cases
Establish Involvement in Crime	12	23.1%
Establish If Crime Committed	7	13.5%
To Gather Evidence	11	21.2%
To Identify Other Suspects	1	1.9%
Suspect Asked What Would Happen	6	11.5%
Statement of Suspect	14	26.9%
Development of Conversation	1	1.9%

The full statistical analysis of the variables associated with interviews outside the police station is reported in Table B in Appendix III. The statistical procedures adopted here were identical to those for *questioning*. The analysis showed that only three variables were linked to interviews outside the police station. These were the age of the suspect, the presence of other people at the time of arrest and the existence of any other suspects.

The occurrence of interviews was related to the age of the suspects. Juveniles were rarely ever interviewed outside the police station (just 2 of the 104 juvenile suspects were interviewed) whereas interviews were carried out in 9% (49) of cases involving adults (x^2 = 8.218; d.f. = 1; p<.005).

The presence of other persons at the time of arrest was also linked to interviews (x^2 = 15.324; d.f. = p<.005). Interviews also were more likely when the suspect was arrested in the presence of family or friends (in 15% of such arrests) and most unlikely (in fact no cases were found), when two or more suspects are arrested at the same time. This last finding is hardly surprising as officers probably will not interview suspects jointly, or within possible hearing of each other, for obvious tactical reasons. In fact, when there are other suspects the incidence of *interviewing* declines (x^2 = 6.342; d.f. = 1; p<.05). When there were other persons believed to be connected with the alleged offence the incidence of interviewing declined. When there were no other suspects interviews took place in 11.5% of cases, as compared to only 5% when there was another suspect. This suggests that, whenever there are others thought to be connected with the offence, the police prefer to clarify their respective parts in the incident in separate interviews at the police station.

There was a statistically significant interaction between the location of arrest, ethnic group of the suspect and interviews outside the police station ($x^2 = 11.549$; d.f. = 3; $p<.01$). When suspects were arrested at home, about 26% of non-Caucasians were interviewed, as compared to only 6% of Caucasians. When arrests were made in the street, Caucasians were more likely to be interviewed (15% of cases as compared to 6% for non-Caucasians).

Non-offence related conversations outside the police station

Officers reported having had extensive conversations with suspects in 43 cases (5.5%), limited conversations in 163 cases (25.4%). Conversations that were restricted to the minimum necessary for politeness occurred in 223 cases (34.8%) and in 220 cases (34.3%) officers reported having had no non-offence related conversations whatsoever. These figures are of interest, if only for the fact that police officers often claim to make what are colloquially called "deaf and dumb" arrests, in which arrest and caution are said to take place without eliciting a reply from the suspect, with "no other conversation" taking place. This appears to be merely a convenient fiction, at least in a significant proportion of cases.

In the questionnaire the officers were asked whether or not any of these non-offence related conversations had been tape recorded. The results showed that in 42 cases (6.6%) tape recorders were used. Although it is not possible to state with certainty that the only reason for the use of tapes was self-protection (see Chapters 1 and 2), this is the most probable motive for the use of tapes. Given the nature of the survey it is likely that this last figure represents a highly conservative estimate of the frequency with which officers are using tape recorders, particularly since officers were asked about the use of tape recorders solely in relation to non-offence related conversations.

Cases in which suspects were interviewed, questioned and with whom officers held extensive conversations were rare. In only four cases did such a combination arise. In a further 11 cases there were interviews, questioning and limited conversations. Occasions in which all three forms of police-suspect encounter occur are, therefore, very scarce.

There were three notable patterns in the data concerning non-offence related conversations. Firstly, non-offence related conversations were held much more frequently (41% of cases) when the suspect was arrested at home, rather than at the station (27% of cases), at the crime scene (also 27% of cases) or in the street (24% of cases). Secondly, conversations were more common where detectives made arrests (41%) than where they were made by uniformed officers (29%). Thirdly, arresting officers were more likely to have conversations with adult suspects (about 32% of cases) than with juveniles (20% of cases).

4
THE CHARACTER OF *INTERVIEWS* OUTSIDE THE POLICE STATION

This Chapter focuses on the 52 cases in which suspects were interviewed outside the police station, looking specifically at the evidence obtained. The Chapter is divided into two main sections, the first looking at the outcomes of the interviews and the methods of recording the statements. The second section looks at the actual records of interviews.

Evidence obtained during *interviews* outside the police station

Table 11 below shows the outcomes of the 52 interviews conducted outside the police station. In one case data were missing.

Table 11
The outcomes of *interviews* outside the police station

Outcome of *Interview*	Number and Percentage of Cases
Full confession (facts and intent)	21 (41.2%)
Admit facts, denial of intent	8 (15.7%)
Other damaging admission	9 (17.6%)
Said nothing at all	0 (0.0%)
Denied that offence occurred	5 (9.8%)
Denial, no alibi	2 (3.9%)
Denial, with alibi	4 (7.8%)
Other Offences	2 (3.9%)
Missing	1 –
Total	52

There were a high number of confessions and admissions amongst the sample of 52 cases, with nearly three quarters of suspects making some form of admission. This rate is higher than the rate of admissions obtained when interviews take place inside the police station where confessions and admissions occur in only about 59% of cases (see Table 12). Although no suspects said nothing at all, four of the 52 suspects (7.7%), each of who denied the allegations against them, used their right of silence during these interviews. In two cases the outcome of the interview was ambiguously recorded as "other offences".

The high confession/admission rate outside the station can be explained by making reference to the reasons why interviews took place (see Table 10). Apart from the cases in which an *interview* was conducted when *questioning* would have been more appropriate, there are three main reasons for interviews outside the station. These can be summarised as follows:

i. Some suspects may be classified as 'confessers'. Although one cannot be certain that there were no prior exchanges with the police, some interviews appear to have been initiated following an earlier statement by the suspect. These suspects may be more likely than other suspects to make spontaneous confessions. The sample of suspects interviewed outside the police station is therefore not truly representative, to the extent that it is a self-selecting group.

ii. Some suspects appear to engage in bargaining. Another reason for the initiation of interviews is a question from the suspect, in which they ask what is going to happen. In Irving's (1980) research such a request was seen as a willingness on the part of the suspect to enter into negotiations (or bargaining) over the content of their future statement and the likely outcome of detention. For example, a suspect might state "I'll admit it if I can have bail". The officer's response to this request for information may have a bearing on the outcome of any subsequent interview.

iii. Police officers are specifically seeking confessions or other information at the time of arrest. Some interviews are carried out to "gather evidence". These may be either important cases or simply those in which officers want to obtain an early admission. The ambiguous nature of the explanation "to gather evidence" makes it difficult to clarify why officers deemed an interview to be necessary. This particular problem will be discussed more fully at the end of this Chapter.

Of the 52 interviews a surprisingly high number, 32 cases (61.5%), were *not* contemporaneously recorded. In only one case (1.9%) was the record made on a designated contemporaneous notes form, whilst in the other 19 cases (36.5%), records were made in officers' pocket books. In these 32 cases it is at least possible that records were made after arrival at the police station.

In 15 of the 20 cases when records were made prior to arrival at the police station, suspects were given a chance to check the record (prior to arrival at the station) and of these 15 cases the record was signed in 11 cases. Six of the interviews were tape recorded, although this fact did not seem to form part of the official record of the interview. In summary, of the 52 interviews, records were ostensibly kept, checked and then signed prior to arrival at the police station in only 11 cases. These results were not exclusively associated with any one police force.

It should be noted that the outcome of interviews was not related to who initiated the interview. When the interview was classified as having been started by a *police officer*, in 15 of the 20 cases (75%) suspects made some form of admission or damaging statement, with the remaining five suspects each denying the accusation. In the cases in which the *suspects* started the interview, exactly the same proportion of admissions and damaging statements resulted, that is, 21 of the 28 suspects (75%) in this category made some form of admission. In these cases six suspects denied the accusation, with one outcome being classified as "other offences". In the three cases in which *another person* was seen as initiating the interview, there were two admissions, and one case outcome labelled as "other offences". How an interview started does not appear to be related to the outcome of that interview. There is a high number of admissions regardless of who opened the interview.

The content of *interviews* conducted outside the police station

Copies of the written records of interviews were collected for 15 of the cases in which interviews took place outside the police station. In this section the contents of these interviews are summarised.

The first thing that is apparent from reading the records of interviews is that they are almost always very short and contain very little in the way of recorded exchanges. In several cases the content of the actual interview is a single statement made by the suspect, for example, "I hit him". Most of the relevant details concerning the offence under investigation are given in the narrative leading up to the suspects' statements, which are also usually covered only briefly. The reasons for conducting interviews are rarely stated in the records. If the research questionnaire had not asked the reason for some interviews, it would have been impossible to determine why the interview took place. Even with some form of explanation available, it is still difficult to see why many of the interviews began. In several cases the questions that were put appear to be unrelated to the offence under investigation, relating instead to other possible crimes ("other offences"). For example, in one case a suspect was questioned about the theft of a child's bike. According to the officer's pocket book, where the record of interview was made, the suspect denied any knowledge of this incident and was then arrested (and *then* cautioned) in connection with the separate theft of a motor bike. No questions about this second offence appeared on the record of interview. In this last case there appears to be no legitimate reason for the interview to have taken place.

Another striking aspect of some of the interview records is that they are unreadable. In one case it is impossible to decipher quite what a suspect appears to be admitting to having stolen.

The records of interviews contain a variety of scenarios which admit of more than one interpretation. In one case where a suspect was found in possession of drugs, he apparently asked the arresting officer if he could "throw away" the heroin. In another case where a suspect was arrested in connection with a building society robbery, prior to being searched in the custody suite, the suspect is said to have asked the arresting officer if he could "have a word" with him. The officer declined. The suspect then produced over £2000 from his pockets which, when asked where it had come from, he admitted to having stolen from a building society.

In another interview the reason for conducting an interview is curiously missing. It is a good example of how the need for *interviewing* may apparently arise outside the police station. A suspect had been stopped in his car for an unspecified reason. The arresting officer saw a craft knife under the steering column. The officer said "I propose to search your car for an offensive weapon because I see something that looks like a knife". The suspect was then cautioned and asked why he had the knife, to which he replied that he was a cab driver and he kept the knife for protection. At this stage the suspect clearly felt he was being picked on and said, "Look just because a Sergeant got stabbed today don't hassle me". When arrested the suspect just said "Typical" and subsequently, according to the arresting officer, became aggressive when he was placed into a police car. In this case the arresting officer presumably decided that the possession of a knife was in itself sufficient to justify interviewing the suspect to seek evidence of *mens rea*.

Another interesting example illustrates the progress from questioning to interviewing. Two police officers in a patrol car saw a man walking along the street. The man was carrying a coat under his arm, and the officers thought this odd because it was extremely cold that day. When the man turned and saw the police car, he dropped an object from inside the coat. This created a loud metallic clanging noise, but the man carried on walking. One officer stopped the man whilst the other retrieved the dropped object, which turned out to be a crowbar. The suspect was asked why he had dropped the object to which he allegedly replied, "I don't know". The man was then asked what he had dropped, to which he replied "a work tool", but when asked what job he did, he said that he was unemployed. The suspect objected to one officer's suggestion that there was only one reason for carrying a crowbar – to break into houses – allegedly saying, "It's only to do a shop, I wouldn't do a house". The suspect was promptly cautioned and arrested, upon which he restated his intention to only, "do a shop, not a house". Several interviews followed this basic pattern of stop, question, detain and interview.

In this study officers were asked to state why interviews outside the station took place (see Table 10). However, ordinarily officer are not required to specify why an interview took place. An improvement on current practice might be to require officers to include the reason for carrying out an interview in their written records. The absence of such a directive is somewhat curious. The Codes of Practice specify that interviews can only be carried out under certain circumstances (C:11.1), and that details of when the interview took place, duration, breaks etc. (C:11.5) must be recorded. However, there is no requirement to justify (in writing) the reason for the interview. Without such a rule it is quite possible that officers will invent post-hoc explanations for why interviews took place.

5
INTERVIEWS INSIDE THE POLICE STATION

Chapter 5 is divided into four sections. In the first section the overall pattern of results concerning interviews inside the police station is described. The case characteristics that might predict the outcome of interviews inside the station are considered, including the variables of questioning prior to arrest, interviews outside the police station and non-offence related conversations (see Chapter 3). In the second section the links between different the statements made by suspect outside the police station are compared to those made inside the police station. In the third section the effects of encounters outside the police station and the decision to seek legal advice are discussed. In the fourth section we consider the link between encounters outside the police station and the decision to charge or release suspects. The statistical analyses relating to this Chapter are reported in Appendix IV (Tables C, D and E).

The outcomes of interviews inside the police station

Of the 641 suspects in this study, data concerning interviews inside the station were collected in 631 cases (there were 10 cases of missing data). In 73 cases suspects were not interviewed inside the police station, leaving a total of 558 (87%) in which interviews inside the police station were conducted.

Of the 558 suspects who were interviewed inside the police station 355 (63.6%) did not receive legal advice, 78 (14%) received legal advice prior to the interview and 125 (22.4%) were interviewed in the presence of a legal representative. 554 (99.3%) of interviews were conducted in a designated interview room, whilst 4 took place in other offices inside the police station. Tape recording was used with 524 suspects (93.9%), video recording with 25 suspects (4.5%) and contemporaneous notes with only 9 suspects (1.6% of cases). 482 suspects were interviewed only once (86.4%), 57 (10.2%) were interviewed twice and 19 (3.4%) were interviewed three times. Table 12 below shows the outcomes of the 558 interviews inside the police station.

Table 12
The outcomes of interviews inside the police station

Outcome of Interview	Number and Percentage of Cases	
Full confession (facts and intent)	222	39.8%
Admit facts, denial of intent	72	12.9%
Other damaging admission	34	6.1%
Said nothing at all	32	5.7%
Denied that offence occurred	47	8.4%
Denial, no alibi	104	18.6%
Denial, with alibi	47	8.4%
Total	558	

Over half of the suspects interviewed in the police station made some form of admission. 32 suspects said nothing at all, while a further 104 denied committing an offence, but did not provide answers that established some form of alibi.

Table 13 below shows the incidence of the right to silence in each of the three forces, including both "selective" and "total" employment of silence.

Table 13
The incidence of the right to silence in each police force

Force	Number of Cases With Interviews	Number and Percentage of Cases In Which Silence Was Used	
Cumbria	269	37	13.8%
Bedfordshire	189	20	10.6%
Metropolitan	100	22	22.0%
Total	558	79	14.2%

There were quite marked variations in the use of silence between the forces. Suspects in the Metropolitan Police sample were twice as likely to use silence as those from Cumbria. Interestingly, the incidence of silence in the Metropolitan sample is higher than that reported by Moston et al. (1992b) of 16%.

The factors associated with admissions inside the police station were analyzed using log linear analysis. The results of this analysis are included in Appendix IV, Table C. This analysis showed that 5 variables had an independent link to the outcome of interviews inside the station. These were: interviews outside the station; non-offence related conversations; legal advice; direct evidence and circumstantial evidence. There was no apparent link between *questioning* and the outcome of interviews inside the station, admissions were as likely to be made whether or not such *questioning* had occurred.

Interviews outside the police station and the outcome of interviews inside the police station

There was a link between interviews conducted outside the police station and the outcome of those conducted inside the station (x^2 = 12.095; d.f. = 2; p<.005), which is shown in Table 14 below. Outcomes of interviews inside the station have been collapsed into three categories, confessions/ admissions, saying nothing, and denials. Suspects who had been interviewed outside the station were highly likely to make admissions in the station and far less likely to deny an accusation. Only 18% of those who are interviewed outside the station fail to admit their guilt inside the station. The corresponding figure for those who are not interviewed outside is 43%. On the face of it, the case both for carrying out such interviews and for recording them is very strong indeed.

Table 14
Interviews outside the police station and the outcome of interviews inside the police station

	Number and Percentage of Outcomes of Interviews Inside the Police Station		
Interview Outside Station	Admission	Said Nothing	Denial
No Interviews	292 (56.8%)	29 (5.6%)	193 (37.5%)
Interviews	36 (81.8%)	3 (6.8%)	5 (11.4%)

Non-offence related conversations outside the police station and the outcome of interviews inside the police station

The links between conversations held on the way to the police station and the outcome of interviews is shown in Table 15. The Table shows that the more extensive the non-offence related conversations, the higher became the number of subsequent admissions (x^2 = 14.685; d.f. = 6; p<.05).

Table 15
Non-offence related conversations outside the police station and the outcome of interviews inside the police station

	Number and Percentage of Outcomes of Interviews Inside the Police Station					
Non-Offence Conversations	Admission		Said Nothing		Denial	
No Conversation	91	47.9%	14	7.4%	85	44.7%
Minimum Conversation	123	61.8%	12	6.0%	64	32.2%
Limited Conversation	92	63.9%	6	4.2%	46	31.9%
Extensive Conversation	23	82.1%	1	3.6%	4	14.3%

There are two possible explanations for this result, centring on who initiated the conversation. It may be that some suspects are, for reasons of personality, more likely to 'chat' with police officers. These 'friendly' suspects are perhaps more inclined to make admissions because they want to please the interviewing officer (raising concerns over certain forms of false confession, see Gudjonsson and MacKeith, 1988). Another possibility is that something said by officers during non-offence related conversations may be having an effect on subsequent interviews. For example, officers may make comments about the possibility of bail or offer other inducements. A less worrying possibility might simply be that officers use the time prior to arrival at the police station to engage in "rapport building" and that they are especially likely to attempt this with those suspects against whom the evidence seems strongest. Rapport building is often advocated on police interview training courses as a means of gaining the cooperation of a suspect, but it is very rare to ever see any such conversations appearing on taped interviews (see Moston, 1992). Whichever of these or other possible hypotheses applies, each confirms the inadequacy of tape recording inside the police station as a wholly accurate record of all relevant verbal exchanges between suspect and interviewer.

The provision of legal advice was also associated with the outcome of interviews inside the police station, replicating Moston et al. (1992a) (x^2 = 18.172; d.f. = 2; p<.0001). When no legal advice was taken suspects made confessions/admissions in about 63% of cases. When legal advice was given prior to the interview the rate fell to 56% and when the legal representative was actually present during the interview it fell to 48%. The percentages of suspects saying nothing were 3% (with no legal advice), 7% (legal advice prior to interview) and 13% (legal representative present).

Two forms of evidence, circumstantial and direct, were also associated with confessions inside the police station. With circumstantial evidence denials were very prevalent (59% of cases) and admissions scarce

(36% of cases), as compared to cases without this evidence (denials in 30% and admissions in about 64% (x^2 = 28.909; d.f. = 2; p<.0001). Direct evidence (such as being found in possession of stolen goods was strongly linked to admissions (x^2 = 25.905; d.f. = 2; p<.0001). When there was direct evidence the association between non-offence related conversations and admissions inside the police station disappeared.

There was a statistically significant interaction between interviews outside the police station, legal advice and the outcomes of interviews inside the police station (x^2 = 7.859; d.f. = 2; p<.05). When there was no interview outside the station, those suspects without legal advice made admissions in 60% of cases, those given legal advice prior to the interview inside the station made admissions in 54% of cases, and those interviewed in the presence of a legal representative made admissions in 49% of cases. When there had been an interview outside the station the pattern of admissions changes. Suspects interviewed without any form of legal advice were highly likely to make admissions (96% of cases), as were those who only received legal advice prior to the interview in the station (100% of whom made admissions). Those suspects who had been interviewed outside the station and received legal advice during the interview inside the station made admissions in about 42% of cases.

There was a second significant interaction between direct evidence, non-offence related questioning and the outcome of interviews inside the station (x^2 = 16.258; d.f. = 6; p<.05). When there was no direct evidence then as the amount on non-offence related conversations increased, so to did the numbers of suspects making admissions (as described in Table 15). However, when there was direct evidence then admissions were made in about 70% of cases for each level of conversation. That is, the extent of conversation was not associated with admissions inside the station.

The degree of correspondence between evidence obtained through interviews outside the police station and evidence obtained inside the police station

There was a high degree of correspondence between statements made outside the station and those made inside the station. Of the 44 suspects whom the police state were interviewed outside as well as inside the station, 35 gave consistent replies, as the figures in Table 16 indicate. That is, initial admissions or denials were repeated inside the station. Of the remaining suspects, five who had initially denied having committed an offence changed their responses towards admissions. Three suspects who had initially made an admission subsequently declined to say anything about the offence (using their right of silence) and one suspect changed from an admission to a denial.

Table 16
Statements inside and outside the station

	Outcome of Interviews Inside the Station		
Outcome of Interviews Outside the Station	Admit	Deny	Neither
Admit	30	1	3
Deny	5	5	0
Neither	0	0	0

In 19 cases in which suspects had been interviewed outside the police station, tapes of the subsequent interviews inside the police station were collected. It had initially been intended that an analysis of the content of these two sources of information would be examined to determine how the officer, or the suspect, made links between the two interviews. However, in only 5 of the taped interviews was there any direct reference to the existence of the earlier interview. This is somewhat surprising. One might have expected that the earlier statement of the suspect would form an integral part of the taped interview, but this is simply not the case. In the majority of cases an independent observer would not realise that an earlier interview had taken place. This is a potentially alarming finding and needs further examination.

In the five cases in the current sample in which reference was made to earlier interviews, on three occasions it was the interviewing officer who brought up the subject, each time to prompt the suspect to restate an earlier incriminating statement, for example, "You had said there was someone else involved". In another case the suspect was asked why he was prepared to implicate a friend inside the station, when he had earlier claimed to be working alone. The suspect replied as follows, "I was in the back of your car. I was full of nerves. I've never been in the back of a police car before". Replies such as this may partially explain why officers are reluctant to raise the topic of interviews outside the station. If the suspect disagrees with any aspect of the earlier statement the reason for this alteration needs to be defined. Suspects are likely either to suggest that they were nervous or confused, or in the worst scenario for the police officer, to suggest that the admission had been coerced. In either situation the validity of the earlier statement is called into question.

In one of the two cases in which the suspect raised the topic of the earlier interview, the suspect complained that he had not earlier been given an opportunity to deny the allegation. In this case of an assault in a pub, the suspect had claimed that he had been told to, "Shut up", by the pub landlord and the arresting officer. In the other case the suspect said that his earlier admission (made in the custody suite after over £2000 had been found on him, see Chapter 4) was the "obvious thing to do".

The decision to take legal advice

The potential influence of encounters outside the police station is not confined only to the outcome of interviews inside the police station. The decision of whether or not to take legal advice, either prior to or during an interview, might similarly be influenced by any of the forms of encounter outside the police station. Overall, about 14% of suspects who were interviewed inside the police station received legal advice prior to the interview, whilst a further 23% were interviewed in the presence of a solicitor or other legal representative.

The effects of the case variables and forms of police-suspect encounter outside the police station on the use of legal advice was analyzed using log linear analysis. The results of which are included in Appendix IV, Table D.

No form of police-suspect encounter (*questioning*, *interview*, or other conversation), showed any link whatsoever to the decision to take legal advice, either prior to or during questioning. Suspects were just as likely to receive legal advice whether or not they had been *interviewed* or *questioned*, nor was legal advice linked to the degree of non-offence related conversation.

The decision to charge or release

Table 17 below summarises the decisions taken with respect to the charging or releasing of suspects. In about 65% of cases suspects were in some way either charged or detained pending further enquiries.

Table 17
The outcome of detention

Outcome of Detention	Number and Percentage of Cases	
Charge	359	57.3%
Refer to Youth/Comm. section	20	3.2%
Caution	27	4.3%
Report	9	1.4%
Detain Pending Further Enquiries	4	0.6%
Release for Further Enquiries	140	22.4%
Release, No Further Action	72	11.5%
Missing	15	–

The possible links between the three forms of police-suspect encounter outside the police station and the decision to charge or release suspects was examined using loglinear analysis (see Appendix IV, Table D). As with legal advice, the three forms of police-suspect encounter showed no apparent link to the decision to charge or release suspects. Charging, releasing etc. were totally unrelated to whether or not *questioning*, *interviews* or non-offence related conversations had taken place. Of those suspects who made an admission outside the station 76% (29/38) were charged (or some further action was taken). 8 of the 13 (61%) who denied the accusation outside the station were charged.

6
Discussion

Summary of main results

One of the main aims of the present study was to determine the extent to which interviews with suspects were being conducted outside the police station. Such interviews occur in only a small number of cases (about 8%) and in most of these cases the statements (for example admissions) made outside the police station are subsequently repeated during a tape recorded interview inside the police station. Some of the reasons the police gave for interviewing outside the police station were within the requirements set out in the Revised Codes of Practice, although there may well be some confusion concerning the distinction between *questioning* and *interviewing*. Statements such as "to gather evidence" and "statement of suspect" do not necessarily mean that the interviewing officer has complied with the Codes of Practice.

Nearly three-quarters of suspects who were interviewed outside the police station made some form of admission. Some suspects appear to have initiated interviews by asking what will happen in their particular case.

The *questioning* of suspects occurred in nearly a third of all cases. There were marked variations in the extent of *questioning* across the forces studied. Afro-Caribbean suspects were more likely to be questioned than either Caucasians or members of other ethnic groups. However, *interviews* were not linked to the race of the suspect.

If police officers are deliberately using encounters outside the police station to influence the decision making of suspects, then the current study might have expected to find some link between such encounters and the decision to take legal advice inside the police station (see Chapter 1). No such link was found. Suspects were just as likely to seek legal advice either prior to an interview, or to have a legal representative present during an interview, regardless of whether or not *questioning*, *interviewing* or any other conversations had taken place.

Police-suspect encounters outside the police station are associated with what happens during interviews conducted inside the police station. The research shows a link between both (i) interviews and (ii) non-offence related conversations outside the police station and the outcome of interviews inside the station. Of course, such associations can be given different, alternative explanations. However, this finding suggests that it is misleading to suppose that interviews inside the police station somehow stand in isolation from everything that has gone before.

Implications of the current study

There are a number of implications for future developments in how police officers interview suspects, either outside or inside the police station. Three main themes are identified: the possible use of portable tape recorders, future legislation on questioning/interviewing and the use of video technology to record interviews inside the police station.

The use of portable tape recorders

The current study has shown that some officers are already carrying personal tape recorders. The figures given here concerning the incidence of use of such tape recorders (about 6%) are undoubtedly a conservative estimate. Other officers may well be carrying tape recorders, but are reluctant to admit that they are doing so. This may be either because they fear disciplinary action, or merely because they do not view the tapes as being officially relevant. That is, the tape recorders are used to forestall any possible disciplinary actions based on allegations of malpractice. The fact that some officers do already carry tape recorders, no doubt encouraged by articles such as those by Heaton-Armstrong and Wolchover (1991a; see Chapter 1), suggests that should portable tape recorders be issued, then simple arguments against their use, such as "they weigh too much", should not be given a great deal of consideration, since officers are already voluntarily carrying them.

It is suggested here that the use of portable tape recorders would represent a positive step towards improving the treatment of suspects, and should therefore be encouraged. However, the arguments in favour of portable tape recorders are complex. The use of portable tape recorders would undoubtedly improve the quality of information gathered at the time of arrest and prior to arrival at the police station, but perhaps its most important effect would be to improve the quality and validity of interviews conducted *inside* the police station.

One advantage of the regular use of tape recorders to record all exchanges with the suspect (as well as witnesses) is that it would remove some of the current stigma concerning exchanges made outside the police station. The current study clearly shows that discussions (i.e., *interviewing* and other conversations) between the suspect and the arresting officer have a bearing on the outcome of tape recorded interviews. It therefore cannot be argued convincingly that the use of tape or even video recording *inside* the station presents a full picture of police interviewing practices. The taped interview represents only a partial picture of a suspect's exchanges with police officers and could be a stage-managed, and sanitized version of police interviewing procedures taken as a whole.

The key advantage in the provision of portable tape recorders would be to compel recognition of the existence of exchanges outside the interview room. Discussing the topic of interviews outside the police station has a surreal flavour, with some officers living under the pretence that they do not occur. As was stated in Chapter 2, some officers claim that interviews outside the station no longer take place. This belief is reflected in the fact that interviews conducted outside the police station are not referred to by officers in taped interviews and when they are mentioned, it is often with reluctance. One central aspect of the investigative process, namely the general process of questioning and discussion leading to arrest, remains concealed from view, submerged in secrecy and obfuscation. This has occurred because officers are unsure of what to do if the suspect makes any kind of statement. Even if correct procedure is followed and the relevant statements are contemporaneously recorded, checked by the suspect and even signed, officers are then faced with the dilemma of how to use this information.

It is not being suggested that recordings made outside the station should be used to replace formal interviews inside the station. There are a number of advantages to carrying out interviews inside the police station for both the interviewer (e.g. time to prepare) and the suspect (e.g. provision of legal advice). The suggestion is, rather, that recordings of interviews made elsewhere should be available as explanatory, background material that may supplement interviews inside the station. Interviewing, as it naturally occurs in police investigations, is not a one-off event, but a process, and the technology is available for a full documentation of that process to be provided.

The provision of portable tape recorders would not automatically mean an end to arguments over police interviewing practices. There will always be scope for officers to have a quiet word "off the record" and, similarly, for a suspect to argue that the tape recorder was not turned on until after a 'discussion'. In reality, there is simply no practicable way to record or monitor every possible occasion in which a police officer has an opportunity to speak with a suspect, nor should such a demeaning practice be necessary in a properly recruited and trained profession. Nonetheless, using available recording techniques in all reasonable circumstances can only enhance responsible and equally, effective investigative interviewing.

The forensic value to the police of accurate recording of all interviews should not be overlooked.

The use of portable tape recorders should not be confined to *interviews* with the suspect. Early questioning and other non-offence related conversations with the suspect should also be recorded. Portable tape recorders may also become an important tool in the investigative process for the questioning of witnesses. This seems a sensible step forward, since it too would help to remove the current over-emphasis on interviews with the suspect inside the police station, by providing alternative and valuable information at a time when witnesses have the events clearly in mind. Witnesses recorded statements might subsequently be used to check hypotheses, clarify errors and suggest new lines of enquiry. For example, innocent persons may become suspects in investigations following a misleading interview with a witness, and the existence of taped records of interviews with witnesses might subsequently clarify how an investigation became sidetracked.

Questioning and interviewing

The Revised Codes of Practice have sought to eliminate interviews outside the police station, except in certain specified circumstances. With the restrictions on interviewing, *questioning* is given greater prominence. The current legislation makes a distinction between questioning and interviewing. Interviews are recorded, questioning is not, unless some damaging statement or admission is made, which must then be recorded, and the caution administered. Officers are clearly not sure of the circumstances in which interviews are permissible, often citing reasons for interviewing which related more clearly to the circumstances in which questioning would be expected to occur.

Officers do not seem to be fully aware of the distinction between *questioning* and *interviewing*, possibly equating the two terms, and given the concerns over *interviews* outside the police station, officers may err on the side of caution by waiting until they have the use of a tape recorder inside the police station before commencing any form of dialogue. This could possibly lead to number of problems, such as a waste in resources, in that a greater number of suspects are likely to be arrested and then interviewed inside the police station than is strictly necessary. Current training initiatives are trying to offer clarification for officers over the circumstances in which there is a need for them to conduct questioning, and this aspect of training may need further elaboration.(from p. 50)

One obvious omission from the current Codes of Practice is the requirement for officers to state in the record of interview, why the interview took place. In the majority of cases in this study the rationale for interviewing is obscure (e.g., "to gather evidence"). In the absence of any requirement to justify an interview at the time that it occurs, there is considerable scope for interviewers to devise post hoc explanations that meet the criteria set out in the Codes of Practice.

Also missing from the current legislation is any requirement for officers to explain why, following questioning, a person is subsequently arrested. Presumably the questioned person says something that precipitates their arrest, but this information is unlikely to be recorded in detail. The legislation covers incriminating statements only.

The current ambiguities between questioning and interviewing experienced by police officers seems certain to result in a number of legal disputes. For example, an appeal in one recent case, R. v. Cox (*The Independent*, January 5 1993; p.22), centred on the admissibility of statements made by the suspect in response to *questioning*. The appeal court ruled that the questions did in fact constitute an *interview*, since their purpose was to elicit an admission. One important aspect of this case was that the ambiguities of the wording of the Codes of Practice was acknowledged. For example, the Recorder noted that the distinction "was difficult to grasp" and that if applied literally, a number of confusions might arise since the purpose of many interviews was to obtain information from a suspect or to obtain that person's explanation of the facts.

Video taping of interviews inside the police station

In a number of submissions to the Royal Commission it is being suggested that the video taping of interviews with suspects inside the police station represents a major step forward in clarifying what really goes on in police interviews. For example, a joint ACPO Superintendent's Association and Federation Report (Police Review, 29 November, 1991; p.2366) advocates video as a "tool to show the truth". That is, video "is the means to invite the court into the interview room to see for themselves the truth of what goes on". In that submission it is even suggested that the use of video would counter calls for confessions to be corroborated.

The current report casts doubts on the prime urgency of the current calls for video technology as a means of accurately portraying police interviewing practices. As we have seen, it is important to regard the suspect's eventual statement inside the station as a result of a series of exchanges between that person and police officers. It is not solely determined by the content/style of the interview inside the police station. The introduction of video inside the station should not necessarily take precedence over the recording of the full sequence of exchanges between police and suspect.

Video technology also has potential dangers that are not widely recognised. For example, it is assumed that jurors will be able to make inferences from observations of a suspect's body language, such as that person is being deceitful. One consistent finding in the psychological literature is that observers are notoriously bad at reading body language and detecting deceit is, realistically, impossible. It has also been shown that where and how the camera is focused will in itself strongly influence the impressions that observers have of a suspect (Lassister and Irvine, 1986). The future use of video technology as a reliable method of validating the interview process is not a straightforward issue.

Future research

The current study was conducted in a relatively short space of time. At the time that this report was completed it was unlikely that many of the suspects who had been charged with criminal offences would have come to trial. It would clearly be of interest to conduct a follow-up study at a later date to see how the cases have fared. For example, it may be that the Crown Prosecution Service (CPS) makes greater use of information derived from interviews outside the police station than do police officers themselves. That is, even though interviews conducted outside the station do not seem to have any independent effect on the decision to charge or release, they may influence the chances of the CPS continuing with a prosecution. Or it may be that cases with evidence obtained away from recording equipment are less likely to reach court. That is, the CPS may feel that given the current concerns over evidence obtained in interviews outside the police station and the wider lack of perceived credibility over confession evidence, that to base any prosecution on such evidence would stand only a limited chance of securing a conviction.

It may also be that some of the suspects in this sample will make allegations of police malpractice following their encounters outside the police station. These allegations may relate to either questioning, or interviewing or to other conversations. The 641 cases in this study are a relatively representative sample of criminal cases and would provide an ideal baseline from which to establish the factors that are associated with allegations of malpractice.

Conclusion

This study has shown that in a large number of cases suspects are questioned, interviewed, or have other conversations with police officers prior to their arrival at the police station. In most cases there is no record of the content of these exchanges and even when records are ostensibly kept, they are typically inadequate. Even under ideal circumstances, contemporaneous notes are not suited for encounters outside the police station and there are strong arguments in favour of the provision of portable tape recorders.

Encounters outside the police station are important for understanding why suspects make admissions inside the police station. Interviews inside the police station, either recorded on audio or video tape, contain only one part of the relevant exchanges between the suspect and police officers. The current legislation, by emphasising the importance of interviews inside the police station has resulted in a situation in which evidence gathered outside the station is seemingly of minimal value. It is widely assumed that the use of tape or video recording equipment inside the station gives a complete picture of the interview with a suspect. This assumption appears to be incorrect. The statements made by suspects on tape are the outcome of a series of conversations with police officers. The interview inside the police station is merely the final part of this process.

References

Baldwin J. (1985) The police and tape recorders. *Criminal Law Review*, 695–704.

Baldwin J. (1990) Police interviews on tape. *New Law Journal*, May 11, 662–663, 681.

Dixon D., Bottomley K., Cole C., Gill M. and Wall D. (1990) Safeguarding the rights of suspects in police custody. *Policing and Society*, 1, 115–140.

Greaves A. and Pickover D. (1991) The conduct of interviews. *Police Review*, 29 March, 652–654.

Gudjonsson G.H. and MacKeith J.A.C. (1988) Retracted confessions: Legal, psychological and psychiatric aspects. *Medicine, Science and the Law*, 28, 187–194.

Heaton-Armstrong A. (1989) An end to verbals. *Police Review*, 7 July, 1376–1377.

Irving, B.L. and McKenzie, I.K. (1988) *Regulating Custodial Interviews: The Effects of the Police and Criminal Evidence Act 1984. Volume I*, The Police Foundation, London.

Irving, B.L. and McKenzie, I.K. (1989) *Regulating Custodial Interviews: The Effects of the Police and Criminal Evidence Act 1984. Volume II*, The Police Foundation, London.

Kinnear P.R. and Gray C.D. (1992) *SPSS/PC+ Made Simple.* Lawrence erlbaum Associates: Hove.

Lassiter, G.D. and Irvine, A.A. (1986) Videotaped confessions: the impact of camera point of view on judgements of coercion *Journal of Applied Social Psychology*, 16, 268–276.

McConville M. and Morrell P. (1983) Recording the interrogation: Have the police got it taped? *Criminal Law Review*, 158–162.

McConville M., Sanders A. and Leng R. (1991) *The Case for the Prosecution.* Routledge: London.

Moston S. (1992) Police Questioning Techniques in Tape Recorded Interviews With Criminal Suspects. To appear in *Policing and Society.*

Moston S., Stephenson G.M. and Williamson T. (1992a) The effects of case characteristics on suspect behaviour during police questioning. *British Journal of Criminology*, 32, 23–40.

Moston S., Stephenson G.M. and Williamson T. (1992b) The incidence, antecedents and consequences of suspect's use of the right to silence. To appear in *Criminal Behaviour and Mental Health.*

R. v. Brezeanu and Francis at *Criminal Law Review*, 650–651.

R. v. Cox. *The Independent*, Jan 5 1993, p.22.

R. v. Vivian Parchment at *Criminal Law Review*, 290–293.

Sanders A. and Bridges L. (1990) Access to legal advice and police malpractice. *Criminal Law Review*, 494–509.

Tendler S. (1992) Camera shy. *Police Review*, 13 March, 482.

Williamson, T M. (1990) *Strategic Changes in Police Interrogation: An examination of police and suspect behaviour in the Metropolitan Police in order to determine the effects of new legislation, technology and organisational policies* PhD Thesis: University of Kent.

Wolchover D. and Heaton-Armstrong A. (1991a) The questioning code revamped. *Criminal Law Review*, 232–251.

Wolchover D. and Heaton-Armstrong A. (1991b) Cracking the codes. *Police Review*, 12 April, 751–753.

Zander, M. (1979) 'The investigation of crime: a study of cases tried at the Old Bailey', *Criminal Law Review*, 203–219.

APPENDIX I

Questionnaire Form A:
Details of Arrest and Characteristics of the Suspect

Form A was completed by the arresting officer in each case. The form was completed either immediately upon arrival at the station, or as soon as practicable afterwards. Form A was divided into five sections (labelled Sections A to E).

At the start of the form details to identify the case such as custody record number, force, station and rank of arresting officer were requested. Section A (*Details of Suspect*) included questions about the sex, age, ethnic group and employment of the suspect; indications of mental handicap; and previous criminal history. Section B (*The Offence and Arrest*) focused on details of the offence, such as offence type(s) and perceived severity; location of arrest; others present at the time of arrest, such as solicitors, appropriate adults, or any other persons; the grounds of suspicion against the suspect at the time of arrest; and whether or not any other persons were known/believed to be involved in the offence.

Section C (*Questioning the Suspect for Information Prior to Arrest*) began with an extract from the revised Codes of Practice (Notes for Guidance 11A) stating that "Questioning a person only to obtain information or his explanation of the facts or in the ordinary course of the officer's duties does not constitute an interview". This statement was included to ensure that officers were clearly aware that the questions in Section C were solely concerned with questioning.

There were three questions in section C. The first was, "Prior to the arrest, was the suspect questioned about the offence?". If questioning had taken place there were two supplementary questions concerning where the questioning had taken place and the purpose of questioning.

Section D (*Interviews with the Suspect*) also began with an extract from the revised Codes of Practice stating that "...an interview is the questioning of a person regarding his involvement or suspected involvement in a criminal offence or offences".

The first question in Section D was in three parts and asked whether or not (prior to arrival at the police station) an interview had been initiated by a police officer, or the suspect or by other means. If an interview had taken place a series of supplementary questions were to be completed. These included the location of the interview; the reason for the interview; use of contemporaneous notes; use of tape recording; the use of the right to silence by the suspect; an assessment of the evidence obtained during the interview (e.g., admission); and opportunities for the suspect to check and sign the record of interview. The section concluded with a request that a copy of the record of interview was to be attached to the questionnaire.

The final part of Form A, Section E (*Additional Comments*), included three questions. The first two were concerned with the extent to which other conversations on non-offence related matters had taken place and whether or not such conversations had been tape recorded. The final question was a request for any additional comments concerning questioning or interviewing in the case.

Questionnaire Form B: Interviewing of Suspects Inside the Police Station

This second Form was concerned with the interviewing of suspects inside the police station. Details of every interview with the suspect were to be recorded separately. Space was provided for details of up to three interviews. If more than three interviews took place then officers were requested to continue on a specifically designed continuation sheet (Supplementary Form B) which was available from the custody officer. A copy of Supplementary Form B is included in Appendix II.

Form B included questions on the following: the rank of the primary interviewing officer; the provision of legal advice; the presence of an appropriate adult; method of recording the interview; use of the right to silence; and the interviewer's assessment of the evidence obtained during the interview.

Questionnaire Form C: The Decision to Charge or Release the Suspect

The final part of the questionnaire was completed either by the interviewing officer, or more commonly by the custody officer, after a decision had been reached on whether or not to charge the suspect.

The questions in Form C included the type of action to be taken against the suspect and the importance of interviews in influencing this decision. The final question was in nine parts and asked if the case against the suspect (i.e., those against whom some further action was to be taken) relied on any of the following factors: 1. Interviews conducted outside the police station; 2. Interviews conducted inside the police station; 3. Direct evidence (e.g., found in possession of stolen goods); 4. Independent eyewitness evidence; 5. Eyewitness evidence from a victim; 6. Eyewitness evidence from police officers; 7. Circumstantial evidence; 8. Information from other suspects; 9. Other evidence.

APPENDIX II

Royal Commission on Criminal Justice

Survey on Interviews With Suspects Inside and Outside the Police Station

The Royal Commission on Criminal Justice has requested a survey concerning interviews with suspects in criminal investigations. The survey covers ALL interviews with suspects, including interviews inside and outside the police station. The aim of the study is to collect information on how often suspects are questioned, where interviews take place and the type of information that is elicited.

The survey is separated into three forms. The questionnaire should remain attached to the custody record until all three have been completed.

Form A: Details of Arrest and Characteristics of Suspect

This Form is to be completed by the arresting officer for every suspect brought into custody.

Form B: Interviewing of Suspects Inside the Police Station

This Form is to be completed by any officer who interviews the suspect in the police station.

Form C: The Decision to Charge or Release the Suspect

This Form is to be completed by the interviewing officer or the custody officer after a decision has been reached on whether or not to charge the suspect. Please use discretion when completing this Form.

FORM A: DETAILS OF ARREST AND CHARACTERISTICS OF SUSPECT

(To be completed by the arresting officer)

Date:
....

Police Force:
....

Police Station:
....

Rank of arresting officer:
....

Custody Record Number:
....

SECTION A: DETAILS OF SUSPECT

1. Sex of Suspect (tick one)

[ ] Male
[ ] Female

2. Age of Suspect (in years)

[ ] years

3. Ethnic group of suspect (tick one)

[ ] Caucasian
[ ] Afro-Caribbean
[ ] Indian/Pakistani/Bangladeshi
[ ] Oriental
[ ] Other

4. Is the suspect employed? (tick one)

[ ] No
[ ] Yes
[ ] Unknown

5. Do you know/have reason to believe the suspect to be mentally disordered or mentally handicapped? (tick one)

[ ] No

[ ] Don't know/not sure
[ ] Yes (please state grounds for belief)

....

6. Does the PNC search reveal previous convictions? (tick one)

[ ] No
[ ] Yes

SECTION B: THE OFFENCE AND ARREST

7. What is the *main* suspected offence? (please specify)

....

8. Other suspected offences (please specify)

....

9. How do you rate the seriousness of the offence? (tick one)

[ ] Trivial
[ ] Moderately serious
[ ] Serious (inc. serious arrestable offences)

10. Where was the suspect arrested? (tick one)

[ ] At station
[ ] At or near scene of crime
[ ] At suspect's home
[ ] Elsewhere (please specify)

....

11. Was a solicitor or other legal representative present? (tick one)

[ ] No
[ ] Yes

12. Was an appropriate adult present? (tick one)

[ ] No
[ ] Yes

13. Was any other person present? (tick one)

[ ] No

[ ] Yes (please specify)

....

14. Grounds of suspicion against suspect before arrest (tick any that apply)

[ ] Earlier statement(s) of suspect
[ ] Direct evidence (e.g., found in possession of stolen goods) or forensic evidence
[ ] Independent eyewitness evidence
[ ] Eyewitness evidence from victim
[ ] Eyewitness evidence from police officers
[ ] Circumstantial evidence
[ ] Information from other suspects
[ ] Information from informant
[ ] Other (please specify)

....

15. Are any other persons other than the suspect known/believed to be connected with this offence (tick one)

[ ] No
[ ] Yes

SECTION C: *QUESTIONING* THE SUSPECT FOR INFORMATION *PRIOR* TO ARREST

> Note: Questioning a person only to obtain information or his EXPLANATION of the facts or in the ordinary course of the officer's duties does not constitute an interview" (Notes for Guidance, 11A).

16. Prior to the arrest, was the suspect *questioned* about the offence? (tick one)

[ ] No (Go to question 19)

[ ] Yes (Go to question 17)

17. Where did questioning take place? (tick one)

[ ] At station

[ ] At/near the scene of the crime
[ ] At suspect's home
[ ] Elsewhere (please specify)

....

18. What was the initial purpose in questioning the suspect? (tick any that apply)

[ ] To establish whether or not a crime had been committed
[ ] To eliminate suspect from enquiries
[ ] To establish whether or not suspect was a witness
[ ] Other (please specify)

....

SECTION D: *INTERVIEWS* WITH THE SUSPECT

Note: Under the Codes of Practice (Revised Edition 1991) an INTERVIEW is the "questioning of a person regarding his INVOLVEMENT or suspected involvement in a criminal offence or offences (Notes for Guidance 11a).

19. Prior to arrival at the police station was an interview initiated by .... *(answer all three parts)*

a. **A police officer** (tick one)

[ ] No [ ] Yes

b. **Spontaneous comments of the suspect** (tick one)

[ ] No [ ] Yes

c. **Other means** (tick one)

[ ] No [ ] Yes (please specify)

....

If you have answered NO to all three questions, please go to question 28.

If you have answered YES to any of the questions, please complete the remaining questions in Section D.

20. Where did the interview take place? (tick one)

[ ] At/near scene of crime
[ ] In police car/van
[ ] In station (not in interview room)
[ ] Other (please specify)

. . . .

21. What was the reason for interviewing the suspect at this stage? (please specify)

. . . .

. . . .

22. Was the interview contemporaneously recorded? (tick one)

[ ] No (please specify reasons below)

. . . .

[ ] Yes (please specify where recorded below, tick one)
  [ ] Contemporaneous note form
  [ ] Pocket book
  [ ] Other (please specify)

. . . .

23. Was the interview tape or video recorded? (tick one)

[ ] No
[ ] Tape recorded
[ ] Video recorded

24. Did the suspect use the right of silence at any stage? (tick one)

[ ] No
[ ] Yes

25. Interviewing officer's assessment of evidence obtained from interview about MAIN offence (choose one option only)

[ ] Full confession of facts and intent
[ ] Admission of facts, denial of intent
[ ] Other damaging admission/evidence (e.g., statement conflicts, partial admission)
[ ] Suspect said nothing at all
[ ] Suspect denied that offence occurred

[ ] Suspect denied offence, no alibi
[ ] Suspect denied committing offence and indicated alibi
[ ] Other (please specify)

. . . .

26. Has the suspect been given an opportunity to check the record of interview? (tick one)

[ ] Yes (go to question 27)
[ ] No (please specify why no opportunity given, then go to question 28)

. . . .

27. Did the suspect sign the record of interview? (tick one)

[ ] Yes
[ ] No

Please attach copies of all records of interviews conducted outside the police station to this form.

SECTION E: ADDITIONAL COMMENTS

28. To what extent did other conversations with the suspect on *non-offence* related matters take place? (tick one)

[ ] Not at all
[ ] Minimum for politeness
[ ] Limited conversation
[ ] Extensive conversation

29. Was the conversation tape or video recorded? (tick one)

[ ] Not applicable
[ ] No
[ ] Yes

30. If you have any additional comments about this case please include them in the space below (continue on an separate page if necessary).

. . . .

. . . .

. . . .

. . . .

FORM B:
INTERVIEWS WITH SUSPECTS INSIDE THE POLICE STATION

1. Was the suspected interviewed in the police station? (tick one)

[ ] No (Do not complete Form B, go to Form C)

[ ] Yes (Please complete Form B)

Space is provided for details of up to three interviews with the suspect. If more than three interviews are conducted please continue on copies of SUPPLEMENTARY FORM B (available from the custody officer) and attach them to this Form.

First interview with suspect

2. Rank of primary interviewing officer:

. . . .

3. Did the suspect receive legal advice? (tick one)

[ ] No legal advice given
[ ] Yes. Legal advice given before interview, no legal representative present during interview
[ ] Yes. Legal representative present during interview

4. Was an appropriate adult present? (tick one)

[ ] No
[ ] Yes. App. adult for juvenile
[ ] Yes. App. adult for mentally impaired/disordered suspect

5. Where did the interview take place? (tick one)

[ ] Interviewing room
[ ] Other (please specify)

. . . .

6. How was the interview recorded? (tick one)

[ ] Tape recording
[ ] Video recording
[ ] Contemporaneous notes
[ ] Other (please specify)

. . . .

7. **Did the suspect use the right to silence at any stage?** (tick one)

[ ] No
[ ] Yes

8. **Interviewing officer's assessment of evidence obtained from interview(s) about MAIN offence** (choose one option only)

[ ] Full confession of facts and intent
[ ] Admission of facts, denial of intent
[ ] Other damaging admission/evidence (e.g., statement conflicts, partial admission)
[ ] Suspect said nothing at all
[ ] Suspect denied that offence occurred
[ ] Suspect denied committing offence, no alibi
[ ] Suspect denied committing offence and indicated alibi
[ ] Other (please specify)

. . . .

Second interview with suspect

9. **Rank of primary interviewing officer:**

. . . .

10. **Did the suspect receive legal advice?** (tick one)

[ ] No legal advice given
[ ] Yes. Legal advice given before interview, no legal representative present during interview
[ ] Yes. Legal representative present during interview

11. **Where did the interview take place?** (tick one)

[ ] Interviewing room
[ ] Other (please specify)

. . . .

12. **How was the interview recorded?** (tick one)

[ ] Tape recording
[ ] Video recording
[ ] Contemporaneous notes
[ ] Other (please specify)

. . . .

13. Did the suspect use the right to silence at any stage? (tick one)

[ ] No
[ ] Yes

14. Interviewing officer's assessment of evidence obtained from interview(s) about MAIN offence (choose one option only)

[ ] Full confession of facts and intent
[ ] Admission of facts, denial of intent
[ ] Other damaging admission/evidence (e.g., statement conflicts, partial admission)
[ ] Suspect said nothing at all
[ ] Suspect denied that offence occurred
[ ] Suspect denied committing offence, no alibi
[ ] Suspect denied committing offence and indicated alibi
[ ] Other (please specify)

. . . .

Third interview with suspect

15. Rank of primary interviewing officer:

. . . .

16. Did the suspect receive legal advice? (tick one)

[ ] No legal advice given
[ ] Yes. Legal advice given before interview, no legal representative present during interview
[ ] Yes. Legal representative present during interview

17. Where did the interview take place? (tick one)

[ ] Interviewing room
[ ] Other (please specify)

. . . .

18. How was the interview recorded? (tick one)

[ ] Tape recording
[ ] Video recording
[ ] Contemporaneous notes
[ ] Other (please specify)

....

19. Did the suspect use the right to silence at any stage? (tick one)

[ ] No
[ ] Yes

20. Interviewing officer's assessment of evidence obtained from interview(s) about MAIN offence (choose one option only)

[ ] Full confession of facts and intent
[ ] Admission of facts, denial of intent
[ ] Other damaging admission/evidence (e.g., statement conflicts, partial admission)
[ ] Suspect said nothing at all
[ ] Suspect denied that offence occurred
[ ] Suspect denied committing offence, no alibi
[ ] Suspect denied committing offence and indicated alibi
[ ] Other (please specify)

....

FORM C: THE DECISION TO CHARGE OR RELEASE THE SUSPECT

1. What action was/is to be taken following this interview in relation to the MAIN offence? (tick one)

[ ] Charge
[ ] Refer to youth and Community Section
[ ] Caution
[ ] Detain pending further enquiries
[ ] Release for further enquiries
[ ] Release, no further action to be taken
[ ] Other

2. How important was the interview(s) with the suspect in making the decision about proceedings in this case? (tick one)

[ ] No interviews
[ ] Low importance

[ ] Moderately important
[ ] Very important

If no further action is to be taken at this stage, go to question 4
If further action is to be taken please complete questions 3a – 3i.

3. Does the case against the suspect rely on any of the following? (answer every question)

3 a. Interview(s) conducted *outside* the police station (tick one)

[ ] No
[ ] Yes

Please ensure that copies of records of all interviews *outside* the station have been attached to this questionnaire.

3 b. Interviews conducted *inside* the police station (tick one)

[ ] No
[ ] Yes

3 c. Direct evidence (e.g., found in possession of stolen goods) or forensic evidence (tick one)

[ ] No
[ ] Yes

3 d. Independent eyewitness evidence (tick one)

[ ] No
[ ] Yes

3 e. Eyewitness evidence from victim (tick one)

[ ] No
[ ] Yes

3 f. Eyewitness evidence from police officers (tick one)

[ ] No
[ ] Yes

3 g. Circumstantial evidence (tick one)

[ ] No
[ ] Yes

3 h. Information from other suspects (tick one)

[ ] No

[ ] Yes

3 i. Other (please specify)

. . . .

Additional comments

4. If you have any additional comments about the interview(s) in this case please include them in the space below (continue on a separate page if necessary).

. . . .

. . . .

. . . .

. . . .

SUPPLEMENTARY FORM B
(Only to be completed if the suspect is interviewed inside the police station on MORE than three occasions)

1. Custody record number:

. . . .

2. Number of interview (circle one) 4 5 6 7 8 9 10

3. Rank of primary interviewing officer:

. . . .

4. Did the suspect receive legal advice? (tick one)

[ ] No [ ] Yes

5. Was an appropriate adult present? (tick one)

[ ] No [ ] Yes

6. Where did the interview take place? (tick one)

[ ] Interviewing room [ ] Other (please specify)

. . . .

7. **How was the interview recorded?** (tick one)

[ ] Tape recording
[ ] Video recording
[ ] Contemporaneous notes
[ ] Other (please specify)

....

8. **Did the suspect use the right to silence at any stage?** (tick one)

[ ] No [ ] Yes

9. **Interviewing officer's assessment of evidence obtained from interview(s) about main offence** (choose one option only)

[ ] Full confession of facts and intent
[ ] Admission of facts, denial of intent
[ ] Other damaging admission/evidence (e.g., statement conflicts, partial admission)
[ ] Suspect said nothing at all
[ ] Suspect denied that offence occurred
[ ] Suspect denied committing offence, no alibi
[ ] Suspect denied committing offence and indicated alibi
[ ] Other (please specify)

....

APPENDIX III

Statistical Analyses in Chapter 3

After defining the extent of questioning and interviewing outside the police station the next stage of the analysis was to determine the case characteristics (such as age of suspect, rank of arresting officer etc.) linked to each form of encounter. The analysis was carried out using a version of log linear analysis (hierarchical log linear analysis) available on SPSS/PC+. The rationale and procedures for such analyses are outlined in a number of publications (such as Kinnear and Gray, 1992). This analysis determines the extent of associations between categorical variables, such as those featured in this study and reveals the independent effects of variables and any interactions.

In order to facilitate the analysis, for certain variables it was necessary to collapse related or similar responses into smaller, more manageable sets. For example, the different types of offences were categorised into two basic groups, property and person offences. This process can, unfortunately, lead to the disguising of some interesting associations. Therefore, where necessary, supplementary details have been added in the main body of the report to expand on any potentially interesting trends in the data.

In the analyses reported in Chapter 3, the following grouped categories of data were used: *Force* – three categories (Cumbria, Bedfordshire and Metropolitan); *Type of arresting officer* – two categories (uniformed officers and detectives); *Sex of suspect* - two categories (male and female); *Age of suspect* – two categories (juvenile and adult); *Ethnic group of suspect* – four categories (Caucasian, Afro-Caribbean, Asian and others); *Previous convictions* – two categories (no previous convictions and has previous convictions); *Offence* – three categories (property offences, person offences and others); *Severity* – three categories (trivial, moderately serious and very serious); *Location of arrest* – four categories (at station, at crime scene, at home/residence/work/friend's house and in the street, not the crime scene); *Solicitor* – two categories (solicitor absent and present); *Appropriate adult* – two categories (appropriate adult absent and present); *Others present* – four categories (no others present, witness/victim present, family/friends present and other suspect present); and *Any other suspects* – two categories (no other suspects and other possible suspects). The variable of *questioning* had two categories, absent and present.

Table A: Log Linear Analysis of Factors Associated with *Questioning* Outside the Police Station

VARIABLES	df	Partial X^2	Probability
Force	2	37.243	$p<.0001$
Ethnic group of suspect	3	17.421	$p<.001$
Location of arrest	3	10.415	$p<.05$
Any other suspects	1	5.844	$p<.05$
Offence category	2	4.879	n.s.
Type of arresting officer	1	0.682	n.s.
Sex of suspect	1	0.214	n.s.
Age of suspect	1	0.896	n.s.
Previous convictions	1	2.839	n.s.
Severity	2	0.294	n.s.
Solicitor present	1	0.543	n.s.
Appropriate adult present	1	1.996	n.s.
Other persons present	4	4.869	n.s.
Ethnic Group x Any other suspect	1	4.696	$p<.05$

Table B: Log Linear Analysis of Factors Associated with *Interviews* Outside the Police Station

VARIABLES	df	Partial X^2	Probability
Age of suspect	1	8.218	$p<.005$
Other persons present	3	15.324	$p<.005$
Any other suspects	1	6.342	$p<.05$
Force	2	2.901	n.s.
Type of Arresting Officer	1	0.040	n.s.
Sex of Suspect	1	0.130	n.s.
Ethnic Group of Suspect	3	2.776	n.s.
Previous Convictions	1	0.009	n.s.
Offence category	2	1.856	n.s.
Severity	2	0.453	n.s.
Location of Arrest	3	5.900	n.s.
Solicitor present	1	0.001	n.s.
Appropriate Adult present	1	2.397	n.s.
Location of arrest x Ethnic Group	3	11.549	$p<.01$

APPENDIX IV

Statistical Analyses in Chapter 5

The analysis in Chapter 5 focused on the effects of encounters outside the police station and the interviewing of suspects inside the police station, the decision to seek legal advice and the decision to charge or release. To facilitate data analysis the seven possible outcome categories were collapsed into three primary categories: admissions made (including 'full admission', 'admission of facts but denial of intent' and 'other damaging admissions'); suspect said nothing at all; and denial (including 'denying that an offence occurred', 'denial with alibi', and 'denial without alibi').

In addition to the case characteristics used in Chapter 3, the following variables were included in the analysis: questioning prior to arrest (present or absent), interviews outside the police station (present or absent) and non-offence related conversations (present or absent) outside the police station.

The analysis of outcome of interviews inside the police station included only the following general case characteristics: the variables of legal advice, previous criminal history and evidence (based on research by Moston et al., 1992a).

Table C: Log Linear Analysis of Factors Associated with Outcome of Interviews Inside the Police Station

VARIABLES	df	Partial X^2	Probability
Questioning outside the police station	2	4.232	n.s.
Interviews outside the police station	2	12.095	p<.005
Non-offence related conversations	6	14.685	p<.05
Legal advice	2	18.172	p<.0001
Previous Convictions	2	3.283	n.s.
Direct evidence	2	25.905	p<.0001
Circumstantial evidence	2	28.909	p<.0001
Eyewitness evidence	2	1.228	n.s.
Victim evidence	2	1.360	n.s.
Police witness	2	1.344	n.s.
Evidence from other Suspect	2	5.536	n.s.
Evidence from an informant	2	1.394	n.s.
Interview outside x legal advice	2	7.859	p<.05
Non-offence conversations x direct evidence	6	16.258	p<.05

Table D: Log Linear Analysis of Factors Associated with the Decision to Seek Legal Advice Inside the Police Station

VARIABLES	df	Partial X^2	Probability
Questioning Outside the Station	2	1.997	n.s.
Interviews Outside the Station	2	0.678	n.s.
Conversations Outside the Station	6	12.537	n.s.

Table E: Log Linear Analysis of Factors Associated with the Decision to Charge or Release

VARIABLES	df	Partial X^2	Probability
Questioning Outside the Station	2	0.029	n.s.
Interviews Outside the Station	2	0.003	n.s.
Conversations Outside the Station	6	0.388	n.s.

Printed in the United Kingdom for HMSO
Dd296482 7/93 C8 G3396 10170